Jupiter

by Gregory L. Vogt

Consultant:
Ralph Winrich
Aerospace Education Specialist
for NASA

Bridgestone Books
an imprint of Capstone Press
Mankato, Minnesota

Bridgestone Books are published by Capstone Press
151 Good Counsel Drive, P.O. Box 669, Mankato, Minnesota 56002
http://www.capstone-press.com

Library of Congress Cataloging-in-Publication Data
Vogt, Gregory.
    Jupiter/by Gregory L. Vogt.
    p.cm.—(The galaxy)
    Includes bibliographical references and index.
    Summary: Describes the planet Jupiter and its surface features, atmosphere,
rotation and orbit, moons, and more.
    ISBN 0-7368-0512-5
    1. Jupiter (Planet)—Juvenile literature. [1. Jupiter (Planet)] I. Title. II. Series
QB661.V642 2000
523.45—dc21

99-047675

Editorial Credits

Erika Mikkelson, editor; Timothy Halldin, cover designer and illustrator; Kimberly Danger
    and Jodi Theisen, photo researchers

Photo Credits

Astronomical Society of the Pacific/NASA, 6, 8, 10, 12, 18
NASA, cover, 14, 16, 20

1 2 3 4 5 6 05 04 03 02 01 00

Table of Contents

Jupiter and the Solar System 5
Fast Facts 6
The Planet Jupiter 7
Atmosphere 9
Revolution and Rotation 11
Inside Jupiter 13
Rings 15
Collision with a Comet 17
Moons 19
Exploring Jupiter 21

Hands On: Magnetic Fields 22
Words to Know 23
Read More 23
Useful Addresses 24
Internet Sites 24
Index 24

Relative size of the Sun and the planets

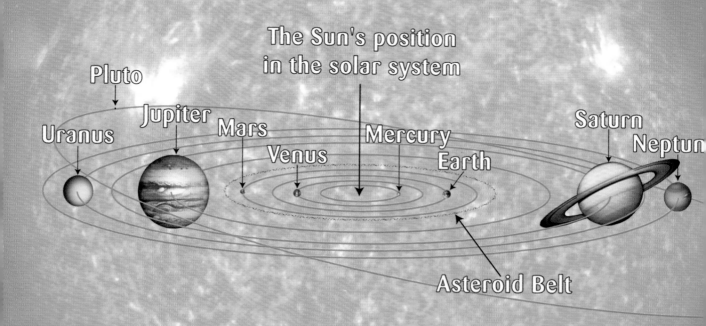

Pluto

Uranus

Jupiter

Mars

Venus

The Sun's position in the solar system

Mercury

Earth

Saturn

Neptune

Asteroid Belt

The Sun

Jupiter is a planet in the solar system. The Sun is the center of the solar system. Planets, asteroids, and comets travel around the Sun.

Nine known planets orbit the Sun. The rocky inner planets are Mercury, Venus, Earth, and Mars. The outer planets are Jupiter, Saturn, Uranus, and Neptune. They are made of gases. Pluto is the last planet in the solar system. It is made of rock and ice.

Jupiter is the fifth planet from the Sun. Like the Sun, Jupiter is a ball of gases. Unlike the Sun, Jupiter is very cold. It is too cold for life as we know it to exist on Jupiter.

This illustration compares the sizes of the planets and the Sun. Jupiter is the largest planet in the solar system. The blue lines show the orbits of the planets. Thousands of asteroids move around the Sun. The asteroid belt is between the orbits of Mars and Jupiter.

FAST FACTS

	Jupiter	**Earth**
Diameter:	88,850 miles (143,000 kilometers)	7,927 miles (12,756 kilometers)
Average distance from the Sun:	483 million miles (777 million kilometers)	93 million miles (150 million kilometers)
Revolution period:	11 years, 350 days	365 days, 6 hours
Rotation period:	9 hours, 55 minutes	23 hours, 56 minutes
Moons:	16	1

Io

Europa

Jupiter is twice as large as the other planets in the solar system combined. Astronomers call Jupiter the giant planet. Jupiter is 88,850 miles (143,000 kilometers) in diameter.

From Earth, Jupiter only is visible at certain times. The planet looks like a bright star. Jupiter and the other planets follow a path called an orbit. The Sun's gravity pulls planets to keep them in their orbits. Jupiter sometimes is behind the Sun and cannot be seen from Earth. Jupiter is easiest to see when Earth is between it and the Sun.

Galileo Galilei, an Italian astronomer and scientist, first studied Jupiter in 1610. He was the first person to look at Jupiter through a telescope. Galileo discovered Jupiter's four large moons.

The space probe *Voyager 1* took this photograph of Jupiter. Two of Jupiter's moons appear in front of the planet. Io and Europa are about the same size as Earth's Moon.

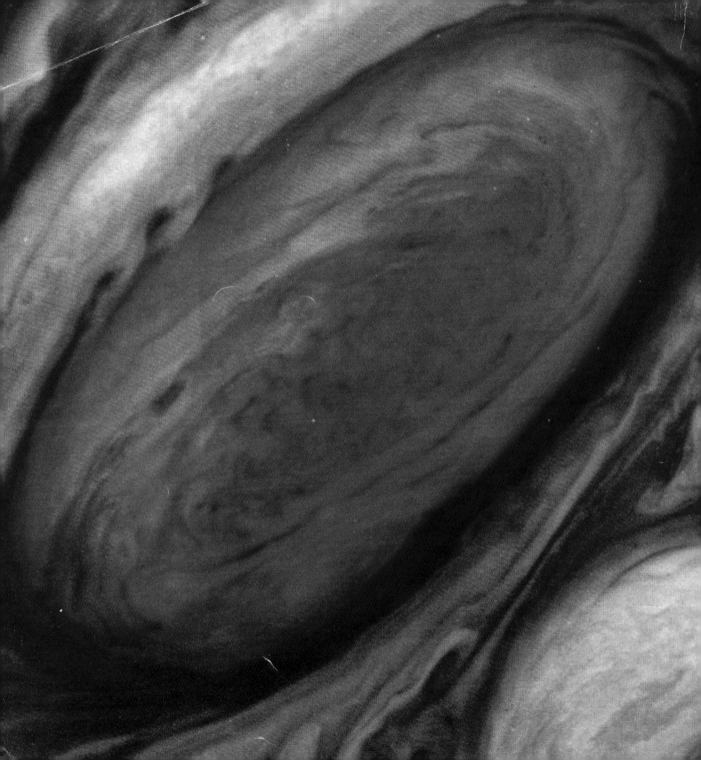

A mixture of gases called an atmosphere surrounds Jupiter. The planet's atmosphere is made of hydrogen, helium, methane, and ammonia.

Jupiter's atmosphere appears as stripes that circle the planet. The stripes are called belts and zones. Zones are white. Belts are orange or red. The colors come from the different gases that make up Jupiter's atmosphere.

A close-up view of Jupiter shows many clouds. Strong winds blow the clouds around Jupiter at a speed of 400 miles (644 kilometers) per hour.

Storms form between the belts and zones. One storm is called the Great Red Spot. This hurricane is twice the diameter of Earth. Observers first saw the Great Red Spot more than 350 years ago.

The space probe *Voyager 2* took this photograph of Jupiter's Great Red Spot.

24 This symbol represents Jupiter. All planets except Earth are named for characters in Greek or Roman myths. In these ancient stories, Jupiter was King of the Roman gods.

Revolution and Rotation

Jupiter and all other planets in the solar system revolve around the Sun. The time of one revolution depends on a planet's distance from the Sun. Earth orbits the Sun once every year. Jupiter is five times farther from the Sun than Earth. Jupiter makes one trip around the Sun about every 12 years.

Planets that are farther from the Sun also move more slowly. The Sun's gravity does not pull as much on these planets. Earth orbits the Sun at a speed of 67,000 miles (108,000 kilometers) per hour. Jupiter moves around the Sun at a speed of 29,000 miles (47,000 kilometers) per hour.

Jupiter rotates as it orbits the Sun. The planet rotates once every 9 hours and 55 minutes. The number of hours and minutes of one rotation is one day on Jupiter.

Voyager 1 took this photograph, which shows the side of Jupiter that is turned away from the Sun. The white areas show lightning in Jupiter's atmosphere.

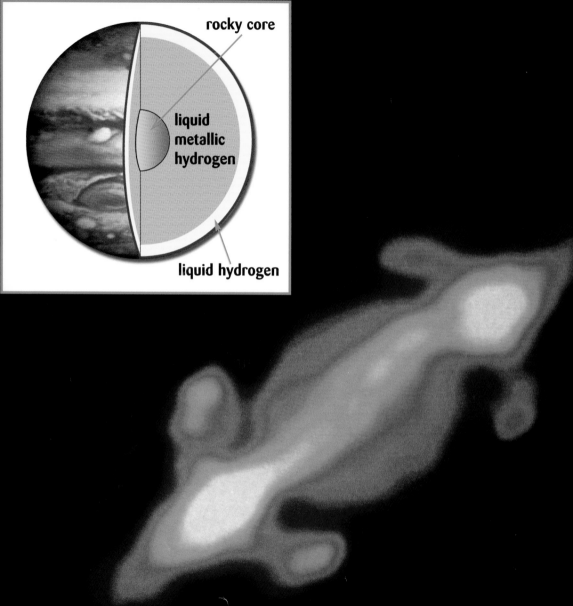

rocky core

liquid metallic hydrogen

liquid hydrogen

Astronomers believe Jupiter's core is made of rock. This core is 15 times the size of Earth. A layer of liquid hydrogen surrounds the core. Above the liquid hydrogen is Jupiter's atmosphere.

Electricity runs through the liquid hydrogen. Heat from Jupiter's core warms small particles in the liquid hydrogen to make electricity. The electricity produces radio waves that can be heard on Earth.

The electricity also creates a huge magnetic field that surrounds Jupiter. This field is very strong and attracts many particles that orbit the planet. The particles become charged with electricity and give off heat in the form of radiation. Jupiter's magnetic field is ten times stronger than the magnetic field that surrounds Earth.

This photograph of Jupiter was captured through radio waves. The colors show Jupiter's strong magnetic field.

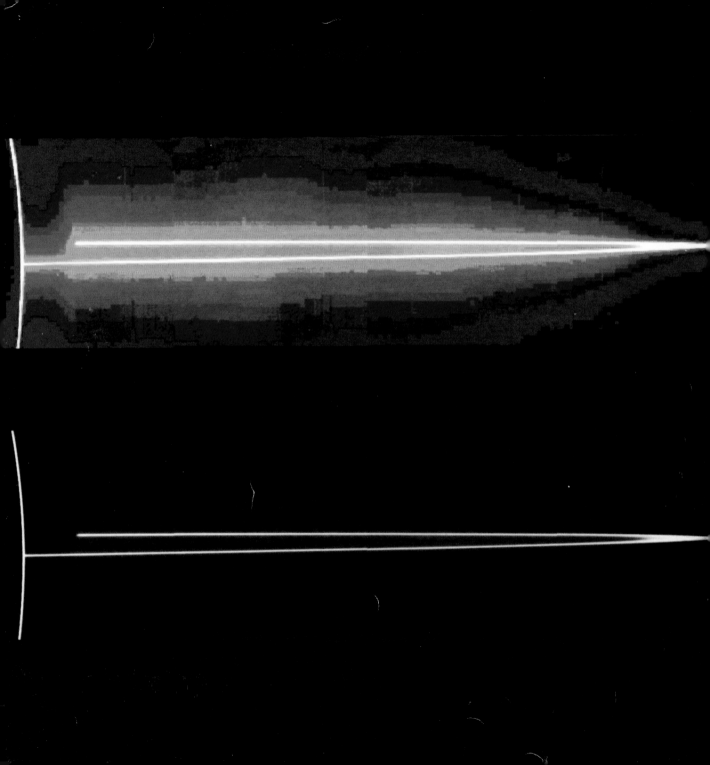

Rings

Jupiter has three rings. Jupiter's rings are very dark. They cannot be seen with ordinary telescopes from Earth. Astronomers discovered the rings when they sent a space probe past Jupiter. The space probe photographed the rings as sunlight sparkled through them.

The rings are made of small pieces of dark rock and dust. This rock comes from Jupiter's four inner moons. Small meteorites strike the moons and create dust. The dust spreads out and forms rings around Jupiter.

Scientists named the rings Halo, Main, and Gossamer. Halo, the smallest ring, lies closest to the planet. Halo is only 114,335 miles (184,000 kilometers) in diameter. Main, the middle ring, is 152,240 miles (245,000 kilometers) in diameter. Gossamer is the largest and outermost ring. It is 160,240 miles (257,874 kilometers) in diameter.

These images show Jupiter's Main ring. The *Galileo* space probe took this photograph in 1996.

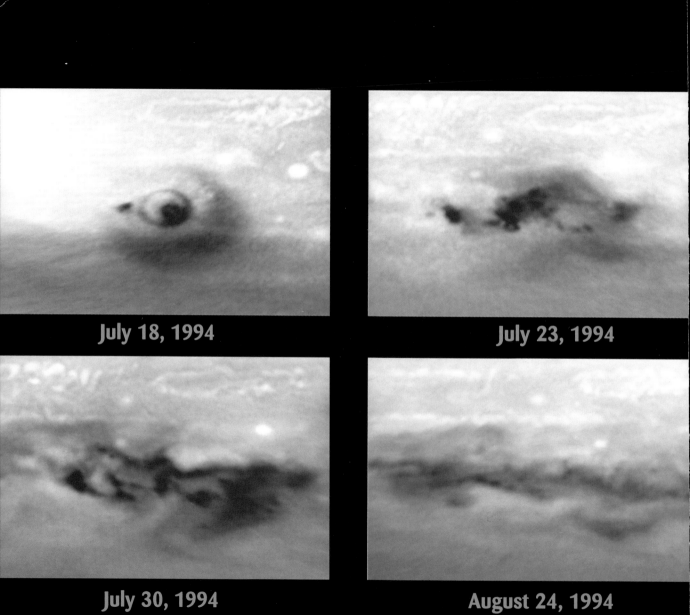

July 18, 1994

July 23, 1994

July 30, 1994

August 24, 1994

Collision with a Comet

In 1993, Comet Shoemaker-Levy 9 passed near Jupiter. Comets are chunks of ice and rock that orbit the Sun. Comet Shoemaker-Levy 9 broke into many pieces when it passed Jupiter. The pieces spread out in a long line. In 1994, the pieces fell into Jupiter's atmosphere one at a time. Each piece fell in a different place.

Astronomers wanted to watch the pieces fall. But the pieces fell on the side of Jupiter that was not facing Earth at the time. Astronomers waited for the spots where the pieces landed to rotate into view. Each piece had created a large dark spot on Jupiter's atmosphere. Astronomers think the comet pieces exploded when they hit the atmosphere.

The *Galileo* space probe photographed a piece of the comet as it fell. The piece was 5 miles (8 kilometers) in diameter.

Pieces of Comet Shoemaker-Levy 9 left scarlike patterns in Jupiter's atmosphere in 1994.

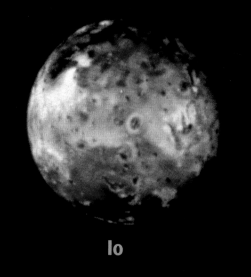

Io

Europa

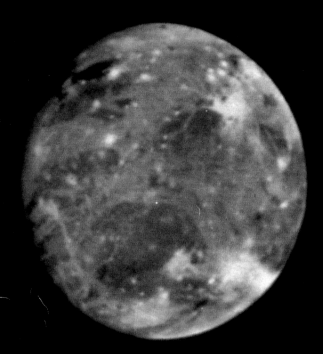

Ganymede

Callisto

Sixteen moons orbit Jupiter. Jupiter's four largest moons are easy to see from Earth through binoculars. They are called Galilean moons because Galileo discovered them.

Ganymede (GAN-uh-meed) is Jupiter's largest moon. Ganymede also is the largest moon in the solar system. It is 3,278 miles (5,275 kilometers) wide. Ganymede is made of rock and ice. The moon's surface has large holes called craters. Meteorites made the craters.

Callisto is Jupiter's second largest moon. Craters cover its icy surface. Astronomers think a salty ocean lies beneath Callisto's surface.

Io (EYE-oh) is the third largest moon. Io is about the size of Earth's Moon.

Europa is the smallest of Jupiter's Galilean moons. Europa's surface is smooth ice. Long cracks appear in the ice. Astronomers believe an ocean of water lies beneath Europa's surface.

This photograph shows the relative sizes of Jupiter's four Galilean moons.

Io

Ganymede

Astronomers have sent six space probes to Jupiter. In 1973, *Pioneer 10* passed Jupiter and sent the first space probe photos of the giant planet. The space probes *Pioneer 11, Voyager 1, Voyager 2, Ulysses,* and *Galileo* also explored Jupiter.

Each space probe carried cameras and radios. The space probes took pictures of Jupiter and its moons to radio to Earth. The space probes also carried scientific instruments. These instruments gathered specific information about Jupiter.

Astronomers used the information from the space probes to learn about Jupiter. They made many discoveries through close-up views from the space probes. *Voyager 1* discovered the rings around Jupiter. *Galileo* gave astronomers information about Jupiter's atmosphere. Astronomers also have used the Hubble Space Telescope to look at Jupiter. This telescope that orbits Earth has taken very clear pictures of Jupiter.

The space probe *Pioneer 10* took this photograph of Jupiter, Io, and Ganymede on December 3, 1973.

Hands On: Magnetic Fields

Jupiter is surrounded by a strong magnetic field that attracts particles orbiting the planet. The magnetic field is stronger at the poles of the planet. You can observe how magnetic fields work by using a small magnet.

What You Need

One 12-inch (30-centimeter) long piece of string
Bar magnet
100 small paper clips
Large bowl

What You Do

1. Tie one end of the string to the center of the magnet.
2. Put the paper clips in the bowl. Hold the magnet over the bowl.
3. Slowly lower the magnet into the bowl.
4. Notice where the paper clips cling to the magnet. Most of the paper clips should be attracted to the ends of the magnet. This happens because the magnetic field is stronger at the poles of the magnet.

Words to Know

astronomer (uh-STRON-uh-mer)—a person who studies planets, stars, and space

atmosphere (AT-muhss-feehr)—the mixture of gases that surrounds some planets

belt (BELT)—a band of dark-colored clouds around Jupiter

diameter (dye-AM-uh-tur)—the length of a straight line through the center of a circle

gravity (GRAV-uh-tee)—a force that pulls objects together

meteorite (MEE-tee-ur-rite)—a piece of rock from space that strikes a planet or a moon

orbit (OR-bit)—the path of an object in space as it travels around another object in space

revolution (rev-uh-LOO-shuhn)—the movement of one object around another in space

ring (RING)—a band of rock and dust that circles a planet

rotation (roh-TAY-shuhn)—one complete spin of an object in space

zone (ZOHN)—a band of white clouds around Jupiter

Read More

Brimner, Larry Dane. *Jupiter.* A True Book. New York: Children's Press, 1999.

Landau, Elaine. *Jupiter.* Watts Library. New York: Franklin Watts, 1999.

Useful Addresses

Canadian Space Agency
6767 Route de l'Aéroport
Saint-Hubert, QC J3Y 8Y9
Canada

NASA Headquarters
Washington, DC 20546-0001

The Planetary Society
65 Catalina Avenue
Pasadena, CA 91106-2301

Internet Sites

The Nine Planets
http://www.tcsn.net/afiner

StarChild
http://starchild.gsfc.nasa.gov/docs/StarChild/
StarChild.html

Index

asteroids, 5
belts, 9
Callisto, 19
clouds, 9
Comet Shoemaker-Levy, 17
electricity, 13
Europa, 19
Galilei, Galileo, 7

Ganymede, 19
Gossamer, 15
Great Red Spot, 9
Halo, 15
hydrogen, 9, 13
Io, 19
Main, 15
zones, 9